For My Grandson Joey - D.H.   for my friend Karen - J.D.

Be PROUD to Be Blue

by **DIANE HULL**
illustrated by **JAN DOLBY**

MacLaren-Cochrane Publishing, Inc.

Text©2021 Diane Hull
Cover and Interior Art©2021 Jan Dolby

Be Proud to be Blue Dyslexic Edition

For information, e-mail the publisher at:

MCPInfo@Maclaren-Cochranepublishing.com

Library of Congress Control Number: 2021933108

First Edition

ISBN
Hardcover: 978-1-64372-369-3
Softcover: 978-1-64372-370-9

For orders, visit

www.MCP-Store.com
www.maclaren-cochranepublishing.com
www.facebook.com/maclaren-cochranepublishing

Baby bird went out to play.
He wanted to play with the fish.
"Hello," said Baby Bird. "Can I play too?"

"But you're blue! We can't play with you!" said the fish, "So please go away."

Baby bird felt very sad,
but went on his way.

Baby bird went out to play.
He wanted to play with the horses.

"Hello," said Baby bird. "Can I play too?"

"But you're blue! We can't play with you!" said the horse, "So please go away."

Baby bird felt very, very sad,
but went on his way.

Baby bird went out to play.
He wanted to play with the frogs.
"Hello," said Baby bird. "Can I play too?"

"But you're blue! We can't play with you!"
said the frog, "So please go away."

Baby bird felt very, very, very sad,
but again went on his way.

Baby Bird sat alone in his tree and watched as the others played.

He looked at his feathers.
"I don't understand what is
wrong with being blue anyway."

He liked being blue. It felt
good to be blue, and he
didn't know how else to be.

So, Baby bird flew back to the fish. "You are orange, and I am blue; that doesn't mean I can't play with you," he said to the fish.

The fish smiled. Then they played in the water, and they became good friends.

Baby bird flew back to the horses.
"You are brown, and I am blue; that doesn't mean
I can't play with you," he said to the horse.

The horses smiled.
Then they played in the
field, and they became
good friends.

Baby bird flew back to the frogs. "You are green, and I am blue; that doesn't mean I can't play with you," he said to the frogs.

The frogs smiled. Then they played on the lily pads, and they became good friends.

Baby Bird wasn't sad anymore, "I'm proud to be blue," said Baby bird.

Diane Hull - Author

Diane Hull is a retired Primary School teacher, specialising in the Early Years, who lives in Todmorden in England. Known as "Grandma Duck" to her grand-children, she is very much in touch with what young children like to read and have read to them. Educated at Manchester Metropolitan University, Diane graduated with a B A (Hons) First Class in Early Childhood Studies and is a member of the Society of Children's Book Writers and Illustrators.

www.dianehull.co.uk

Jan Dolby - Illustrator

Jan Dolby is an internationally published illustrator from Toronto, Canada. She has a Fine Art degree from the University of Guelph and has illustrated over 20 picture books. Her studio The Pink Suitcase is located in her century home she shares with her husband, two children and dachshund Margaret. Jan is a painter, treasure hunter, hockey fan and tiny house lover. Her favourite animated character is Gru.

You can see more of her work at jandolby.com.

What is Dyslexie Font?

Each letter is given its own identity making it easier for people with dyslexia to be more successful at reading.

The Dyslexie font:
1 Makes letters easier to distinguish
2 Offers more ease, regularity and joy in reading
3 Enables you to read with less effort
4 Gives your self-esteem a boost
5 Can be used anywhere, anytime and on (almost) every device
6 Does not require additional software or programs
7 Offers the simplest and most effective reading support

The Dyslexie font is specially designed for people with dyslexia, in order to make reading easier – and more fun. During the design process, all basic typography rules and standards were ignored. Readability and specific characteristics of dyslexia are used as guidelines for the design.

Graphic designer Christian Boer created a dyslexic-friendly font to make reading easier for people with dyslexia, like himself.

"Traditional fonts are designed solely from an aesthetic point of view," Boer writes on his website, "which means they often have characteristics that make characters difficult to recognize for people with dyslexia. Oftentimes, the letters of a word are confused, turned around or jumbled up because they look too similar."

Designed to make reading clearer and more enjoyable for people with dyslexia, Dyslexie uses heavy base lines, alternating stick and tail lengths, larger openings, and semicursive slants to ensure that each character has a unique and more easily recognizable form.

Our books are not just for children to enjoy, they are also for adults who have dyslexia who want the experience of reading to the children in their lives.

Learn more and get the font for your digital devices at www.dyslexiefont.com

Get books in Dyslexie Font at: www.mcp-store.com

2 Share the words Basic language, word repetition, and whimsical illustrations, ideal for sharing with your emergent reader.

Lightning Source UK Ltd.
Milton Keynes UK
UKHW050634010721
386436UK00002B/48